Garden Clippings

poems by

Cynthia Storrs

Finishing Line Press
Georgetown, Kentucky

Garden Clippings

To my father, who taught me to love growing things; to my mother, who taught me to love words; to my husband, who modeled a love of music—all of which I needed to write these poems. And to my children and grandchildren, to remember me. Soli Deo gloria.

ACKNOWLEDGMENTS

"Banking on Futures," in *Poetry While You Wait*, Pikes Peak Library District,
April 2010.
"Everything That Breathes" in *The Tennessee Magazine*, August 2020.
"One Must Not Forget the Promise" in *Messages from the Hidden Lake*, Vol.
V, Literary and Art Collection of Alamosa Public Library, 2013.
"Pot of Dying Tulips" in *Gathering: Work from the Bon Richard Poetry Group*,
2019.

Immense gratitude and appreciation go to my friends of the Bon Richard
poetry group (Colorado Springs): Aaron, Ben, Fawn, Laura, Pat, Price, and
Ron, who collectively encouraged me to publish. You believed in me when I
didn't yet believe in myself.

Thanks as well to Cathy and Ione of the Full Moon Poetry Group
(Tennessee), who also helped workshop a number of these poems.

Publisher: Leah Huete de Maines
Editor: Christen Kincaid
Cover Art: Cynthia Storrs
Author Photo: Alayna Bledsoe
Cover Design: Elizabeth Maines McCleavy

Order online: www.finishinglinepress.com
also available on amazon.com

Author inquiries and mail orders:
Finishing Line Press
PO Box 1626
Georgetown, Kentucky 40324
USA

Contents

A Grain of Mustard

It takes a lot of hope to plant a garden.
First, you have to believe that sun will rise, daily.
You can't have a philandering light source, like the moon.
You need something faithful, dependable, always there
even when you can't see it.
Then, water. You can help here of course
but then again, plentiful fidelity is priceless.
But needfully moderate. Thunderbolts, hail
while flashy and attention-getting
is not the gentle rain required.
Think of bathing a baby. Soft, warm trickle.
Rivulets that tickle. That'll do the trick.

And then your seeds—or young sprouts.
Will the seeds take hold?
Those middle school sprouts
—will they stay the course?
You know how capricious
is pre-adolescence: change
is their only constant.

And what faith we plant in placing
bulbs in the fall. Promises
made over the long haul:
"If you go deep enough,
blanket me, and leave me be
I will dazzle you in early spring."
Who else do we know for only a handful
of minutes, that steadfastly returns
six months later as promised?
There's loyalty for you.

And the earth itself. It opens—
or is violated—and we entrust it,
then trust it, to support
and then release the child
it has fostered, not swallow into oblivion.

I rely on the ground that lies
beneath my feet to remain
level, whole, warm, generous.
I plant this stem to see it flower.
I plant this hope,
to eat its fruit.

January Flowers

Brave, the purple pansies push
aside the snow. Violet veins
pulse through gold. Tiny faces
turn through cold
to golden sunlight,
cover tender, cowering
shoots, greening leaves.
These courageous reminders
reassure me.
Winter, too, will pass.

Pot of Dying Tulips

The leaves are curled
and rise to thin chartreuse peaks
counterpoint to petals
curved like purple gourds
scoops for withheld water
now too late.

Yellow stamens stand erect
while pollen laden pistils
droop in mustard tiredness.

Crisp and brittle
twisted into grotesque purple stars
the blossoms
keep a singular beauty

like my mother's hands—
lined, veined, worn, and beautiful.

February Drear

February's damp, cold grey
vanquished in a single thrill—
today I spied a golden burst:
spring's first daffodil.

Cheekwood Botanical Gardens

A sea of red stood at salute
to greet our ruddy hands and cheeks.
The brisk March wind in full pursuit
as crimson tulips lined the streets.
And shoulder stood with daffodils
their sunshine chased grey clouds away.
A soldiers' cavalcade, they drill
to breeze, bend double time and sway.
White hyacinth sweet scent has won.
Green leaves parade in water's gleam.
Crocus at ease, their duty done,
while bluebells occupy the stream.
Fleet is spring's flamboyant fanfare.
If only time could tarry there!

April Snow in Colorado

the bleached bones of skeletons reach
towards bandages unrolled among the hills
foolscap traps the roofs
while flake-feathered
pine-scented evergreens
sift onto Styrofoam shrubs

the streets are licorice with greasy splotch
mirrors of cement skies
coal-capped chick-a-dee
ensconced in floured fronds
trills, then plucks a red berry

Narcissus

yolk yellow
crenellated cup
egg-time Easter
Star of David
pushing your paper
coat to the edges
of a flattened green pipe
forcing an agnostic
to flower to faith
in springtime again

Last Tulips—a Duplex

Crimson petals bleed down
streaks of red retrace the crown.

The red streaks form a crown
that halo straight and firm green stalks.

The firm green stalks herald spring,
fresh scarlet cups that cradle.

Crimson cradles circle white and point,
anoint our eyes, dancing with light.

Our anointed eyes dance with their light
but now the blossoms splay.

Red blossoms withered, too stiff to play,
their girdled leaves in disarray.

Green-girdled leaves in disarray
as crimson petals bleed down.

Every Thing Breathes in Tennessee

The broccoli hills heave,
their green sheaves hover and hug
the air, cocoon the skin
warm, soft, mouth to mouth
cheek to cheek, like a midnight dance.

Walls breathe in Tennessee.
Corners that have been cleaned
spring to life with millipedes.
From sidewalks that have been swept
spring minuscule shins and shanks,
armies that sting and bite.
Cobwebs take flight overnight.
Every thing breathes in Tennessee.

Every thing breathes in Tennessee.
The striped stream that ripples and curls,
turgid rills and furls, hides the swish of a trout,
(*Oncorhynchus mykiss*) and fat channel catfish.

Every thing breathes in Tennessee.
Foxtail and bittercress, henbit and oxalis
sway and shake, flaunt and undulate.
Restless with the breeze, they tease,
they breathe

as every thing breathes in Tennessee.

Flowers for My Mother

Perusing through produce
pink carnations beckon me.
Memories of Mom.
Whenever she came to visit
I put pink carnations in her room.
They last the longest
—good value for the money, my dad would say.
But she adored them for their exotic
spiciness, their delicate ruffles,
their ramrod straight stems.
Shoulders back, she would tell me:
stand tall. Like the pink carnations—
feminine and proud, enduring and fragrant.

A last memory of her—
hunched in a wheelchair,
shivering, too weak to dress herself.
I wrapped her in a warm
carnation-colored sweatsuit.
So pretty in pink,
the oncologist said.
No longer straight, fragrant,
feminine or enduring,
she winked at the doctor,
still spicy.

Garden Clippings

I go to transplant the gardenia.
Diva of the garden,
it has flagged and failed
royally where I planted it.
Too much sun? Too little water?
I pull it from the ground
a year later, it has hardly rooted.
I sigh and look to shovels.
Tulip shovel, narrow and deep?
Spade, sharp and short?
I stand before the towering, heavy,
wooden long-handled tool
left me by my father. Like him
a workhorse built to last.
I take it from the wall, the heft
balances perfectly in hand.
The smoothness of the shaft,
the weathered place where hands fit.
I know exactly where to hold, how to stand,
where to place my foot and push
to turn the earth and lift, again and again.
I pull it through the grass, my heart catches.

If only you were here to tell me
where and how to plant, how to tend,
what to sow, what to tear out,
what I can ignore and what I cannot.
I feel your hands on mine now
soft and smooth like the wood
you left me. You are leaning on your shovel,
shaking your head at my ignorance.
For all my university degrees,
I can't keep a simple shrub alive.
Water, you say, but not too much—
sunlight, but the right amount—

weed and feed, but only the right ones.
Remember that annual pruning
promotes growth, and be vigilant—
root out any molding, dead stuff.
He speaks of the gardenia, I suppose—
I turn and take the shovel back.

Dandelion (*Taraxacum officinale*)

Snowflake of summer, a snowball of seed
tripping in the wind, lighting where you please,
cursed by gard'ners who only see a weed,
loved by children, on whose breath you are freed.
Millions of suns swaying on seas of green,
preparing for flight, adventures unseen.
When rooted—impossible to upend,
older—untrappable as you ascend.
And I who am mobile, I stand amazed.
This social outcast rides Aeolus' waves.
My species evolved to tie me to earth;
your children fly skyward, in bursting rebirth.
Who am I to disdain this golden bloom?
I rest in place; the world's your fortune.

July

The early morning sky is crystalline
blue, but wet
like a lover's mouth
hovering above my cheeks,
my neck, my chest.
The summer trees,
a row of broccoli crowns
with spectator clouds behind.
These like yeast will expand
and rise throughout the day;
over-proofed, they will explode
this afternoon into thunder.
My black puppy pants
and rolls heels over head
in dewy grass to lick
water from broad blade weeds.
She spirals, slides, and dives
to cool herself, picking
up green lint of yesterday's clippings.
We are hot now.
My lover's fled.
The air is dog breath.
I pass a merlot leaf with one
clear pearl. I think to drink
it. But my dog
is quicker.
We turn to amble home,
too hot to trot. The puppy's
long, pink tongue droops.
The hair on my neck's
a sweaty goop. Birds trill,
the air is still. Summer
morning thrills in Tennessee.

Heaven's Ebb

The trees exhaled a murmuration.
Then, the green breathed back in
and the wave reformed
receded back onto itself,
black into itself.
Amorphous starlings startling
the eye, the passerby,
rinsing tidal pools of clouds in the sky.

August

Cicadas chitter in overblown trees
a dry sound like Western rattlers.
But snakes are below, sliding through streams—
undulating ripples in the cool, the only cool.

Tomatoes have grown to folded fists,
red like bursting hearts, heavy on green vines.
Lettuce has gone to seed; the herbs are weeds.
Susans with black eyes turn blindly to the sun
lavender faints; the pansies live out
their name, wilting in terra cotta
pots on cement.

The rain that drips rises as fetid mist.
Heat wraps me in a fevered sponge.
The dog pants to breathe, listless on the porch.
All that was fresh becomes dun, umber,
and rotting. Pink and white impatiens
turn brown, vines droop to the ground.
Only the bugs can make a sound.

To A Stink Bug, Imprisoned

How did you get trapped
inside my screen? Poor bug.
even your name is disdained,
your fragrance worse.

The only beings who like you
are those who eat you.
How would my days
unfold if I were loved only
by those who consume me?

Definition of domestic violence:
Considered a pest,
you are greeted with disgust.
Swatted when seen,
you keep coming back.

Needing to be nourished,
accepting abuse.
Sensing fresh air,
you may not reach it.

Tea in Tennessee

I ate the last honey from Colorado
a homesick, mountain-missing girl in Tennessee.
I wonder how the honeybees know

as they meander through blue lupine in Otero,
I pulled the final spoonful through a cup of tea.
I ate the last honey from Colorado.

I touched sagebrush buttercup, smelled horsemint, row upon row
a meadow of blossoms that moved like the sea.
I wonder how the honeybees know

through peaks dissecting the sky to find columbine, groves
of trembling aspens gold, burnished by August heat.
I ate the last honey from Colorado

sweet as purple larkspur, and Indian paintbrush aglow
pollen from bluebells, fireweed, and Rocky Mountain bees.
I wonder how the honeybees know.

After fall rains, before cold November snow
find your way through mountain valleys and come east to me.
I ate the last honey from Colorado.
I wonder how the honeybees know.

Labor Day

There is heat yet in the air
but the chevron geese overhead
—harbingers of cooler clime—
remind me that time
is not a circle but spirals on.
False friend,
Time, whose seasons are eternal—
but not I.
I believe the lie
that I too will cycle always,
returning next autumn.

Which link of that chevron
will skip next September?

Nearing Home

The raccoon lay on the side of the road
arranged as if sleeping.
Its eyes half-closed as if drowsing
limbs comfortably crossed
as if in perfect peace and security
lying on its side like my puppy by the fire.
As I sped past I asked
aloud if it'd been struck
and spent its last moments
in pain, inhaling the stench
diesel, asphalt, exhaust.
Or, feeling tired, had it carefully padded
to a stretch of familiar road
and fixed its eyes on the green
hills in the horizon, breathing
in the licorice scent of purple
pickerel weed, of white sweet clover
and suddenly overcome
with fatigue,
decided to stretch itself out
for a final rest.

I hope
my end comes the same,
in intimate community
surrounded by fresh grasses
facing towards a shimmering vista.

The Garden of Colorado Springs
—After Yeats

I will arise and go now to Garden of the Gods
and find no dry-stone fences there by former slaves made.
Instead, a rugged ridge like stegosaurus backs
red thrusting rock, gold aspen glades.

I shall have peace there, dropping in on hawks
drifting in arroyos of cinnamon-scented white pine.
Heat shimmers at noon, cools to silver for moon-lit walks,
night cries of bat and owl in kind.

I have ached to return for four years. I ever see
the lapis blue sky, I grind the red grit in my teeth.
While I'm fond of the broccoli hills of Tennessee,
I miss purple mountains' majesty.

Fireworks in Fall

Those who think fall's an ending are missing the point:
Mother Nature explodes and with brilliance anoints.
Scarlet and ochres, peaches to pink,
then dun turns to brown as she runs out of ink.
The summer sun's furnace cools as it mellows,
that blinding white eye fades to pale yellow.
The air in the morning greets with a bite
and returns with champagne to chill our good night.
Life freshens, then pauses, and takes a deep breath,
then shoulders white robes for a brief pretend death.
Easter is critical, and Christmas—delightful.
but April's just soggy and August is frightful.
Spring, summer, winter—I might just throw over
to live in a land that is always October.

Landscape

Rivers from above falling in cords
outside my studio window.
Grey skies, leaden roofs,
licorice streets, silver ponds,
dusky gloom. A plume
of mist creeps across the grass.
Inside, before me are fireworks of chroma:
a mixing guide, color wheel,
summer clover sketches,
two canvases primed.
Nature and I use similar technique:
a torrid rush or gentle patter
moving liquid across a surface
creating a kaleidoscope
where none existed,
creating a form by first returning it to blank.
I have mentors, have practiced much
and have determined to continue
for the rest of my days.
But I will never match the Master
wielding his wet brush,
stroking the landscape
bringing ordered iridescence
out of nothing, out of chaos, out of void—
which I can but poorly replicate
in the mirror of my canvas.

Banking on Futures

when days go home early
shrugging

when sun dims to bleached ivory
cooling

when listless leaves falter
shattering

when honeysuckle tendrils droop
curling

when sod chills the knees
sinking

I know

this bronze beauty
is a fraud

all will soon be lost
under death's white mask

in defiance
I hide bulbs

banking on their ugly faces
blooming

I know
the market will turn

One Must Not Forget

One must not forget the promise in a frozen garden plot.
The winter garden littered with last season's dead leaves,
dry grass, smooth stones
an upturned pot.
One unharvested bean bush that someone forgot.

But none of this is wasted.
It waits, like the bags of 50/50 fertilizer
for warmer days, gentle rains
and a caring hand

to overturn the clods,
plow under winter's fodder
into the welcoming, warm dark sod underground
the launching pad
for next year's bounty.

Cynthia Storrs self-published her first poetry collection at age nine (and still has the copy). She is currently teaching and writing near Nashville, Tennessee. At the age of 29, she and her husband immigrated to Belgium to work with national churches, where they reared two children who attended French-speaking schools. They remained in Europe for 25 years. A high school and college English instructor for nearly four decades in Europe and the United States, she recently moved to Tennessee from Colorado, where she had served on the board of Poetry West, the Pikes Peak Poet Laureate Committee, and with the Pikes Peak Arts Council, which awarded her a grant by for her work in promoting poetry in the Pikes Peak region. She currently serves on the board of the Poetry Society of Tennessee. Her award-winning poetry has been published in print and on-line in CO and TN; she is listed on the Colorado Poets website. In addition to her poetry, she has published articles on bilingualism, biculturalism, and cultural adaptation and addressed conferences in over ten countries on these topics. She is an amateur painter and regularly incorporates her love for art in ekphrastic poetry. She also enjoys art history, theatre, yoga, and chocolate. Cynthia and her husband Don, along with their dog Rustee, are currently attempting to tame their backyard into a garden. Visit Cynthia at www.poetryandpaintbycyd.com.

Storrs' poems have been published online at *Languageandculture. net* (2010), *The Ekphrastic Review* (2025), *The Paddock Review* (2025); in four volumes of *Messages from the Hidden Lake* (2010, 2011, 2013, 2014); in two volumes of *Poetry While You Wait* (2012, 2014); in six anthologies *(America's Poetic Soul,* 2016; *Gathering,* 2019; *Tennessee Voices Anthology,* 2022-2023, 2023-2024, 2024-2025; *Awakening Within,* 2025); in magazines *Mom Writers Literary Magazine* (2003), *Critique* (2019), *The Tennessee Magazine* (2020), and in the journal *The Awakenings Review* (2025).

Her inspiration for this collection is all of creation, which she believes reflects the glory and wonder of God.

www.ingramcontent.com/pod-product-compliance
Lightning Source LLC
Chambersburg PA
CBHW022059080426
42734CB00009B/1412